Sacramentals

Explaining actions, signs and objects
that Catholics use

by
Fr Richard Whinder

*All booklets are published thanks to the
generous support of the members of the
Catholic Truth Society*

CATHOLIC TRUTH SOCIETY

PUBLISHERS TO THE HOLY SEE

Contents

Discovering Sacramentals

This booklet provides an introduction to the Sacramentals – things and actions through which the Church conveys a blessing. Some of these will be very familiar to most Catholics, whether objects such as rosaries or holy medals, or common gestures such as the Sign of the Cross or genuflection. Others will be less familiar.

An attempt has been made to offer a brief theological introduction to this subject. However, if you are simply looking up information on a particular sacramental, the index provided at the back will take you directly to the page you need.

We have tried to include as many different varieties of sacramental as practical, and to offer adequate information as to their use. Inevitably, there will be omissions. However, we hope the booklet succeeds in its aim, which is to make these riches of the Church better known to our readers.

What is a sacramental?

The Decree of the Second Vatican Council on the Sacred Liturgy, *Sacrosanctum Concilium*, gives us the following definition of sacramentals:

'These are sacred signs which bear a resemblance to the sacraments: they signify effects, particularly of a spiritual kind, which are obtained by the Church's intercession. By them men are disposed to receive the chief effect of the Sacraments, and various occasions in life are rendered holy.'[1]

Sacramentals are distinguished from the seven Sacraments (Baptism, Penance, Holy Eucharist, Confirmation, Ordination, Matrimony, Anointing of the Sick) in two main ways. Firstly, the seven Sacraments were all instituted by Our Lord Jesus Christ during his earthly ministry. They form such a fundamental part of God's plan for us that to receive them is necessary for our salvation (although, obviously, it is not essential for each individual Christian to receive all seven Sacraments). By contrast the *sacramentals* have mostly been instituted by the Church under the guidance of the Holy Spirit. Their number is not fixed, and the Church has the power to institute new sacramentals according to the spiritual needs of the faithful.

Channels of grace

The second main distinction between Sacraments and sacramentals concerns the conferral of grace. Grace is the gift of union with God, first given in baptism. Throughout

---

[1] *Sacrosanctum Concilium*, 60.

our lives we are called to grow in grace, which we do most importantly through the regular reception of the Sacraments; thus we grow closer to God, increase in holiness and are able to practice the Christian virtues more easily. The Catholic Church teaches that in the Sacraments grace is given *ex opere operato* (literally: 'by virtue of the act'). This means that the grace of a Sacrament is caused directly by the action of God, and is not dependent on the worthiness of the human minister nor on the recipient (of course, if we receive the Sacraments with the wrong dispositions – if we put obstacles in the way of God's action – then they will not produce good fruit in us. God will act, but the action will bring us no benefit). With sacramentals the case is different. These are said to work *ex opere operantis* (literally: 'by virtue of the one acting'). This means that any increase in grace will be directly dependent on the dispositions of the one making use of the sacramental. To put it simply, if we use a sacramental superstitiously, carelessly or in ignorance it will do us no good whatsoever.

On the other hand, these sacramentals can be a valuable spiritual tool if used piously, reverently and with understanding. Moreover, using a sacramental is not purely a private devotion. Traditionally, theologians have also spoken of them working *ex opera operantis ecclesiae* ('by virtue of the Church acting'). This means that someone using a sacramental gains more benefit from this than if they had just undertaken a good work on their own initiative – the sacramentals have an efficacy as petitions of the whole people of God, working through the impetratory power of the Church.

One last point should be noted: as we said above, the seven Sacraments instituted by Christ are necessary for our salvation – no Christian can afford to ignore these principal channels of grace. On the other hand, the use of sacramentals is left to our discretion: we can choose among them according to our own devotion. Once again, it is hoped that this booklet, by explaining what sacramentals are and the ways in which we can use them, will encourage individual believers to make use of those sacramentals which are suitable to their state of life and to their own particular needs.

Different types of sacramental

The Church has the power to institute new sacramentals as the needs of the faithful require. This means that, in theory, there could be an almost infinite number of sacramentals. In practice, there are indeed a great number – too many for us to do justice to them fully here. We can only offer an introduction which we hope will be useful. To begin with, let us look at the different types of sacramental which the Church provides. In the early centuries of Christianity, the word 'sacrament' was often used to designate any type of sacred symbol or ceremony (although it was always understood that some were directly instituted by Christ and some not, and that only some were necessary for salvation). The more precise definition between 'Sacraments' and 'sacramentals' derives from the Middle Ages, especially the work of the great scholastic theologians, Peter Lombard and St Thomas Aquinas. At this time, the sacramentals were commonly grouped into six categories, as follows:

- *orans* – prayer
- *tinctus* – use of holy water or blessed oil
- *edens* – eating blessed food
- *confessus* – general confession of sins (as at Mass or in the Divine Office, at Night Prayer)
- *dans* – giving alms
- *benedicens* – blessings, by the Pope, a bishop or priest

A more straightforward approach is to divide the sacramentals into two groups:

- *Things*: covering all blessed objects, such as medals, holy water etc
- *Actions*: liturgical gestures, blessings and exorcisms

This two-fold division is the simpler method which we shall follow in this booklet.

- Sacramental Objects -

Food

Food and drink are essential to our existence as humans - without them we would die. It is not surprising therefore that the Church should encourage us to make use of our meal times both to remind us of our dependence on God, and to foster our human relationships, which are the context in which we live out our journey of faith here on earth.

Grace before and after meals

We should always say grace before and after meals, most especially when sharing food with our family or with friends. In doing so we render thanks to God from whom all good things come, and we remind ourselves that there are others far less fortunate than us, hungry and thirsty in many parts of the world. Saying grace is also a way of inviting God to be part of our meal, and so, part of our lives. The simple act of sharing a meal can create and strengthen all sorts of relationships – not only human, but divine. We remember how in the Bible, from the very earliest times, meals were often seen as having a sacred significance (for example, the meal which Abraham prepared for the three heavenly messengers: *Genesis* 18).

Grace before and after meals can be said by anyone. Most appropriately it is said by the senior person present – the head of the family, or the leader in a community. If grace is said by a priest or deacon they can also bless the food with the Sign of the Cross. When possible, grace should be said aloud, and standing – a simple ceremony to begin and end the meal itself. When this is not possible, the prayers can be said seated and quietly, or even silently. If you are the only Catholic present at a meal you can still say grace silently to yourself and without any outward action – although making the Sign of the Cross (when appropriate) can be a good act of Christian witness in a very secularised world.

The traditional form of grace before meals, most often used by Catholics, runs as follows:

Bless us, O Lord, and these thy gifts
Which we are about to receive from thy bounty
Through Christ our Lord. Amen.

Grace after meals goes like this (it is usual to end with a short remembrance of the Holy Souls, perhaps especially those who have shared our meals in the past):

We give thee thanks, Almighty God
For these and all thy benefits
Who lives and reigns, world without end. Amen.

May the souls of the faithful departed, through the
mercy of God, rest in peace. Amen.

Other blessings of food

In addition to encouraging us to sanctify all our
meals by saying grace, the Church also blesses some
foods at particular times of the year. These blessings
tend to vary very much according to local custom.
For example, at Easter time some places have the
custom of blessing the lamb for Easter dinner – other
places bless eggs. There is also a tradition of
blessing wine on St John's Day (27th December) and
loaves on St Agatha's Day (5th February). All these
customs are very much to be encouraged, for they
have the effect of bringing God into the heart of our
everyday lives.

Fasting and abstinence

As well as encouraging us to bless the food we eat, the
Church sometimes asks us to restrain our appetites through
fasting and abstinence. Fasting means not eating at all (or
eating very little) for a given period: abstinence means
giving up some particular food or drink – traditionally
abstinence for Catholics has meant giving up meat.

Fasting and abstinence have a long history both in
Christianity and in Judaism before it. It is worth noting
that Jesus obviously assumed that his followers would
fast (*Matthew* 9:15, *Mark* 2:20, *Luke* 5:35). Indeed,
almost all religions have found the practice spiritually

useful. We can summarise the benefits of fasting, or abstaining from food we enjoy, in these ways. Firstly, by fasting we are saying 'no' to our physical appetites. As fallen creatures, if we give in blindly to all our desires, they will certainly lead us astray. Exercising self-restraint is a healthy part of being human. Secondly, by allowing ourselves to experience hunger, we unite ourselves in solidarity in some way with those who are deprived, neglected or suffering. Lastly, for the Christian, fasting has a special value: we can unite our voluntary mortification with the Sacrifice of Christ on the Cross, and so, in some tiny way, our own self-denial has a share in the work of salvation.

Rules on fasting

Unfortunately, it is probably true to say that fasting, and self-denial of any sort, are little valued by many Catholics today. The nearest many people get to this concept is 'giving something up for Lent' – and even this is often done rather for health reasons than with any spiritual purpose in mind. Other people have the idea that fasting and abstinence are practices which the Church used to encourage 'in the old days' and that they are outmoded now. In this context it is useful to see what the 1983 *Code of Canon Law* has to say on the subject:

Can. 1249: All Christ's faithful are obliged by divine law, each in his or her own way, to do penance…

Can. 1250: The days and times of penance for the universal Church are each Friday of the whole year and the season of Lent.

Can. 1251: Abstinence from meat, or from some other food as determined by the Episcopal Conference, is to be observed on all Fridays, unless a solemnity should fall on a Friday. Abstinence and fasting are to be observed on Ash Wednesday and Good Friday.

Can. 1252: The law of abstinence binds those who have completed their fourteenth year. The law of fasting binds those who have attained their majority, until the beginning of their sixtieth year…

Can. 1253: The Episcopal Conference can determine more particular ways in which fasting and abstinence are to be observed. In place of abstinence or fasting it can substitute, in whole or in part, other forms of penance, especially works of charity and exercises of piety.

Friday fasting

From the above we can see that the Church by no means considers self-denial to be something which belongs to the past. Put simply, we are all bound to fast (if between the ages of 14 and 60) and abstain from meat every Ash

Wednesday and Good Friday. We are also obliged to do penance on other Fridays of the year (in memory of the first Good Friday when Jesus died for our sins). The precise way in which our Friday penance is to be performed is determined by our local Bishops' Conference. In England and Wales the Bishops have decided that it may be fulfilled in a wide variety of ways:

- by abstaining from meat or some other food
- by abstaining from alcoholic drink, smoking or some form of amusement
- by making the special effort involved in family prayer, taking part in the Mass, visiting the Blessed Sacrament or praying the Stations of the Cross
- by fasting from all food for a longer period than usual and perhaps by giving what is saved in this way to the needy at home and abroad
- by making a special effort to help someone who is poor, sick, old or lonely

It can often happen when you give people too much choice that they become confused, and this certainly seems to have happened with English Catholics as regards the Friday penance – most people now make little or no attempt to fulfil this duty, and many are not even aware that they should.

This is a great shame – and certainly is not the mind of the Church. Indeed, notwithstanding the widespread confusion in this country, it remains the case that we are obliged, by the universal law of the Church, to undertake some definite form of penance every Friday. Not to do so, deliberately and regularly, would even be a sin. It is probably best then, unless we habitually perform some other act of penance, to retain the old custom of abstaining from meat on the Fridays of the year. In this way we can be sure of fulfilling the requirements of the Church, and we make a good act of public witness to our faith. After all, other religions frequently follow quite complex dietary rituals, and are respected for it. Why should we be ashamed to identify ourselves as Catholics in a similar way?

Summary

To sum up: food can have a sacramental value, whether blessed and eaten or given up for a higher purpose. It is not only essential to our physical well-being, but can be a valuable tool in the spiritual life as well.

Water

Like food, water is essential to our earthly life. It is also one of the principal symbols of our Christian faith. Water is used above all in baptism, through which we become Christians and our life of faith begins.

Biblical sign

Throughout the whole history of salvation, water has been a sign of God's saving power. We might think of the description of Creation in the Book of Genesis, when God's Spirit 'moved on the waters' (*Genesis* 1:1). Again, later in Genesis the great flood is a symbol of God's power to make an end of sin, and to give humanity a new beginning: Noah's ark, afloat on the waters, symbolises the Church in which we are saved and faith itself, which is bestowed to us upon the waters of baptism (*Genesis* 6:14). In the Book of Exodus we hear how God led his chosen people through the Red Sea, bringing them to the Promised Land and wiping out their enemies (*Exodus* 14:28). In the New Testament as well, water is a powerful sign of God's salvific action – seen for instance at the moment of Christ's own Baptism in the Jordan, the beginning of his public ministry (*Mark* 1:9). Later, blood and water will flow from his side on the Cross (*John* 19:34) – which the Fathers of the Church see as symbolising the sacraments, flowing from the Heart of the Saviour.

Holy water

Given all this rich imagery, it is little wonder that the Church uses water frequently. It is not only essential to baptism, but, blessed in another form, it becomes holy water. This holy water will in turn be used by the ministers of the Church in performing many other acts of blessing. It can also be used by the faithful for their own private devotions.

Although it is distinct from the water used in baptism, holy water is nevertheless related to it. Ideally, holy water should be blessed on a Sunday, the day of Resurrection, recalling the Easter ceremonies when the font is solemnly blessed and catechumens baptised. In the Extraordinary Form of the Roman Rite, the principal Mass of every Sunday begins with the *Asperges*, or sprinkling of holy water, accompanied by the words of *Psalm* 50: 'washed by thee I shall be whiter than snow' (or in Eastertide, by the words of *Psalm* 117: 'I saw water flowing from the right side of the temple'). This is also an option in the Ordinary Form. Similarly, we will always find stoups (bowls) of holy water just inside the doors of a Catholic church: this too is a reminder of our baptism, through which we entered the Church of Christ. Whenever we enter a church, therefore, we should dip the fingers of our right hand in the holy water and make the Sign of the Cross – not hurriedly and carelessly, but reverently, reminding ourselves of the great gift of faith.

Water used in blessings

How else can holy water be used? As noted above, it is often used by priests and deacons in performing many blessings – for example, blessings of homes, of cars, wedding rings etc. Lay people can also take holy water home with them to use in private devotion. Most churches will have some form of urn or jug where you can easily obtain holy water – it should be taken home in a clean bottle or other vessel used only for that purpose. Once at home, you can place your holy water in a stoup, similar to that in church. Some Catholics like to have a stoup near their front door, to bless themselves on going in or out. Others like to have it near their bed, and bless themselves before going to bed: this is a particularly nice form of devotion for children.

Traditionally salt is added to holy water, to keep it pure and clean for longer. However, if holy water begins to go green, it can of course be poured away: however, you should dispose of it reverently, and always pour it onto clean ground.

Water from Shrines

In a separate category we can place water brought from recognised shrines, such as Lourdes. This is not strictly speaking 'holy water' since it has not been blessed, other than by being in contact with a sacred site. Nevertheless, it can count as a sacramental – and can be used for private devotion in the same way as the holy water described above.

Candles

Like food and water, light is an essential component of life, and of happiness. Christ described himself as 'the light of the world' (*John* 8:12), and the Church frequently makes use of light in her liturgy, notably at the Easter Vigil, with the blessing of the great Paschal candle, and in the liturgy of baptism.

Candlemas

Candles are solemnly blessed on the Feast of Candlemas (2nd February), which recalls the Presentation of Christ in the Temple and Simeon's prophecy that this child would be 'a light to enlighten the gentiles' (*Luke* 2:32). On this occasion the faithful carry candles in procession – these can afterwards be taken home. Traditionally they were then lit during storms; we might update the tradition by lighting them during family prayers, or burning them beside a favourite holy image or statue.

St Blaise

Candles are also used in giving the Blessing of St Blaise, on the day following Candlemas, 3rd February. Here, the priest lays crossed candles on the throat of each person being blessed, and invokes the aid of the saint against 'all disease of the throat and every other evil.'[2]

Votive lights

Most Catholics will be familiar with votive lights – small candles lighted in church in front of the images of Christ, Our Lady and the Saints. These candles are a small offering to the holy people we wish to honour – when we have left the church they will carry on burning, a silent continuation of our prayer.

Candles at Shrines

An extension of this idea can be seen in the votive candles lighted at shrines. These can often be very large, perhaps presented by a parish group or local community in remembrance of its pilgrimage. At such pilgrimage sites candles can often be carried in procession (as at the famous torchlight procession in Lourdes). As with water from these holy places, people often like to take home candles with them, either those they have used in prayer or those bought separately (shrines in German speaking countries, in particular, often sell very beautifully decorated candles which people can buy as a souvenir).

---

[2] St Blaise once saved the life of a boy choking on a fish-bone, and hence is protector of throats.

These again can be used in private devotion at home – perhaps lighted on the anniversary of your pilgrimage, prolonging its memory and effect in your everyday life.

Candle for the dying

One final use of blessed candles may be noted: it used to be the custom to light a candle when someone was close to death, during the prayers for the commendation of a soul. Nowadays, when most people pass their last hours in hospital, this is often impossible. Nevertheless, it is a beautiful custom and should be kept up wherever possible. The senses are often dimmed when close to death, and the bright light of a candle, an eloquent symbol of Christ our Light, might be the last thing that a person sees, and a great source of comfort. Similarly, wherever possible, a candle should be lighted if a priest or minister visits your home with Holy Communion for the sick.

Palms and Ashes

Palm Sunday Procession

Palms and ashes are the subjects of two solemn blessings during the liturgical year. On Palm Sunday, at the beginning of Holy Week, palms are blessed to recall Christ's triumphant entry into Jerusalem, when the crowds laid palms at his feet. The blessing used in the Ordinary Form of the Mass links our own use of palms to the joy felt by the crowd on that occasion:

Almighty God we pray you bless these branches... Today we joyfully acclaim Jesus our Messiah and King. May we one day reach the happiness of the new and everlasting Jerusalem by faithfully following him...

One of the prayers used in the same celebration in the Extraordinary Form adds another dimension, as well as illustrating the Church's belief in the value of all sacramentals:

O God, who, in the wonderful ordering of your creation, have been pleased to use even inanimate things to illustrate the manner of our salvation, grant, we beseech you, that the devout hearts of the faithful may comprehend the mystical significance of what was done this day, when the crowd, inspired by heavenly light, went forth to meet their Redeemer... The palm branches anticipate his victory over the prince of death...

Nowadays the palms are usually dried palm leaves, often sent from the Holy Land. They can be folded to make a small cross, although it is better (and certainly more symbolic) if this is not done till after the service is over. It used to be common to use any local greenery to serve as palms for the procession, and this is still common in Mediterranean countries, where olive branches are used for the purpose – this certainly adds to the colour and verisimilitude of the ceremonies. Having been blessed the palms are held during the procession and again for the reading of the Passion. They can be taken home afterward and kept there reverently, perhaps tucked behind a crucifix, as a reminder of Holy Week.

From palms to Lenten ashes

If you need to dispose of old palms you could offer them to your priest, since, by tradition, last year's palm is burnt to provide the ashes given each Ash Wednesday at the beginning of Lent. Wearing ashes, like sackcloth, has a long tradition in the Bible as a sign of repentance and humility (for example, the King of Nineveh in the Book of Jonah: *Jonah* 3:6). As such they are a suitable 'badge' with which to begin our Lenten journey. In marking our foreheads with the ashes the priest expresses our need for humility in these or similar words: *Remember, man, that you are dust, and to dust you shall return.* After we leave the church, we leave the ashes on our foreheads until they wear off naturally from the course of the day's activities. This is a simple but profound acknowledgment of our faith – and again, a good witness to an unbelieving world.

It is interesting to note that Ash Wednesday (although it is not a Holiday of Obligation) and Palm Sunday are two of the most popular feasts in the liturgical year, and sometimes attract even non-practicing Catholics to church. This is a good indication of the powerful effect the sacramentals can have.

Oil

In the Bible

In the Bible, oil is seen as a sign of celebration and gladness (*Psalm* 103:15), and as a sign of spiritual strength (even today, athletes use oil in exercising and honing their muscles). In the Old Testament it was used to anoint priests, prophets and kings – its use is also recorded by the apostles in the New Testament, particularly in the anointing of the sick (for example, the clear instructions given by the Letter of the Apostle *James* 5:14). Today, we find three sacred oils which are blessed solemnly by the bishop at the Chrism Mass on Maundy Thursday, and are used henceforth in the celebration of the Sacraments. These are the oil of Chrism (used at Baptism, Confirmation and Ordination), of Catechumens (used at Baptism), and of the Sick (used by priests to anoint those seriously ill).

In the Liturgy

It is important that no other oil is used in private devotion, or in para-liturgical celebration, which might be confused with these three oils, solemnly blessed by the Church and set apart for use in the Sacraments. Nevertheless, we do sometimes encounter other types of oil which can be classed as sacramentals. A notable example would be the oil of St Walburga. This is a clear liquid (not strictly speaking oil at all, but known as such) which seeps from the tomb of the English nun, St Walburga (+777) who is buried at Eichstadt in southern Germany. The oil is collected by the nuns of the convent in which the tomb is situated and is given to people coming on pilgrimage. It can be used in private devotion or kept as a memento of pilgrimage. Many miraculous cures have been attributed to this oil, even down to modern times.

Sacred Images

Doctrinal background

Humanity has always valued the images of those it loves and venerates. Images remind us of the people represented – relatives, friends, heroes, benefactors. In ordinary life, people treasure family photographs and pictures of loved ones. In worship, images and statues are used in many of the great religions of the world. In Christianity, this use of images is firmly based upon the doctrine of the Incarnation. In Christ, God the Father has given us the perfect image of himself, through the coming of the God-made-Man. 'To have seen me is to have seen the Father,' says Jesus (*John* 14:9). In Jesus, God literally took on a human form, a human body: he communicated with us through the world of sense. 'That which we have seen with our eyes, which we have looked upon and touched with our hands…that we proclaim unto you' writes St John the Apostle (1 *John* 1, 1-3).

Catechetical value

The astounding fact of the Incarnation modifies the prohibition on the use of images found in the Old Testament and contained in the Ten Commandments

(*Deuteronomy* 5:6-21). The *idolatrous* use of images is indeed a sin – but it is right and proper if we use them to remind us of Christ, the perfect image of the Father, and of his saints, who are, through grace, 'images' of Christ and point us to him, drawing us closer to the mystery of the Godhead. Above all, the proper use of sacred images has a deep catechetical value – they touch the heart, ensuring that our faith does not remain simply on the level of words but draws in the whole person. The Second Council of Nicea in 787 – condemning the so-called 'Iconoclast heresy' which sought to destroy all religious imagery– defended the use of images in these words: 'When people look at images, they are led to happy remembrance of the "prototype", before whom they bow in honourable greeting… He who bows before an icon, bows before the person represented in it'.

Icons and statues

The Council's language reminds us that in the East, up to this day, the image most favoured has been the 'icon', a two-dimensional image on a gold background, in which every detail has its own tradition and interpretation. In the West, at least since the early Middle Ages, we have become more used to three-dimensional statues (this is not to say that icons are unknown in the West: in Rome, many of the most treasured images in the ancient basilicas are icons – such as the famous '*Salus Populi Romani*' of St Mary Major, which tradition has attributed to St Luke).

Proper approach to sacred images

The doctrinal background to the use of sacred images leads to two important considerations. Firstly, we must always remember that in honouring an image we are honouring the person it represents. If we light a candle to the Sacred Heart, or bring flowers to Our Lady, it is in fact an expression of reverence and love for the person depicted. To pay too much attention to the image itself, considered as an image, would be to misunderstand and misuse it.

Secondly, if sacred images actually represent Christ and his saints to us, and if (properly used) they have the ability to lead us closer to them, it follows that these images must be truly worthy of their purpose. We may quote the words of Canon J. O'Connell, a great liturgical expert of the mid-twentieth century:

'Images are part of sacred art, i.e. art which is not merely Christian, not merely religious, but art which is directly and in due manner employed in the service of God's House and in divine worship … Accordingly, images placed in churches should be distinguished from images in general by "a holiness that shuns the profane, truly artistic correctness...and a universality which, while respecting legitimate local customs, manifests the unity of the Church".[3]

There are many different types of image in use among Catholics. Here we will look at just a few.

The Crucifix

This is the most important image in any Catholic church (or school, or home). It represents our Saviour, Jesus Christ, in his supreme act of friendship to mankind, when he died on the Cross to redeem us. 'Greater love has no man than this, that a man lay down his life for his friends' (*John* 15:13).

There are various different types of crucifix. For the celebration of Mass, when the Sacrifice of Calvary is made present on the altar, Church law requires a crucifix which represents the sufferings of our Redeemer (*General Instruction of the Roman Missal*, 308). Other popular types include the 'San Damiano' crucifix (copies of the one which spoke to St Francis of Assisi, asking him

---

[3] J. O'Connell, *Church Building and Furnishing*, Burns and Oates, London, 1955, p. 94. O'Connell is quotong from the Encyclical of Pius XII, *Mediator Dei*.

to 'rebuild my Church') and the *Christus Rex*, which depicts the Saviour in regal and sacerdotal robes. Once again we may quote Canon O'Connell: 'The ideal crucifix expresses the resignation, nobility and serenity of the Crucified, inviting sorrow, confidence and love.'[4]

Our Lady

As with the crucifix, any Catholic church (or school, or home) worthy of the name will have an image of the Blessed Virgin Mary. She is not only the Mother of the Lord (*Luke* 1:43) but also the most faithful of believers (*Luke* 1:38). We need both her maternal intercession and the shining example of her holiness. There are very many different images of Our Lady, many based on local custom or tradition. Some of the most popular are connected with her various apparitions throughout the centuries: Walsingham (England, 1061), Guadeloupe (Mexico, 1531), Lourdes (France, 1858) and Fatima (Portugal, 1917).

The Saints

Different churches will contain the images of various different saints, again depending on local custom, devotion and tradition. A very common image is that of St Joseph, husband of Mary and protector of the

[4] *Ibid*, p. 103.

universal Church. Before all these statues in church it is normal to have a stand for votive candles, which we have referred to above.

Nativity crib

Certain images are particularly associated with the seasons of the Church's year.

Throughout Christmastide most churches will have a crib, depicting the Infant Jesus at Bethlehem. The tradition is believed to go back to St Francis of Assisi, who instituted the first crib at Greccio in 1223.

Stations of the Cross

Another example and Franciscan tradition is the devotion known as the Stations of the Cross, in which the faithful process around the church while meditating on Christ's sorrowful journey to Calvary. It became very popular due to the preaching of St Leonard of Porto Maurizio (+1751) who erected the Stations of the Cross at the Coliseum in Rome. Strictly speaking, the Stations only require fourteen small crosses placed at regular intervals around the walls of a church; in practice, it has become the universal custom to provide fourteen pictures, showing the different stages of Christ's Passion, in order to help those making the devotion to focus their minds. A few churches now add a fifteenth Station – the Resurrection –

although there are times when it would be inappropriate to use it (for example, during Lent, or above all on Good Friday).

Easter Garden

Similarly, some churches construct an Easter Garden, with flowers and plants placed around an empty tomb, to adorn the church at Eastertide. This is a custom which appears to have arisen in Protestant churches, although many Catholic churches in continental Europe place a figure of the Risen Saviour above the High Altar or tabernacle for the whole of the Easter season.

Relics

Distinct from sacred images but related to them, relics are also used to foster devotion to Our Lord and his Saints. Relics, of course, are not mere representations of holy people, but objects tangibly connected to them.

Distinct classes of relic

A First Class relic is a part of a body of a saint (or of the True Cross), a Second Class relic is an object used by them (such as a habit, or rosary) and a Third Class relic is an object which has been touched by another relic. Relics may not be used for public devotion without being certified for the purpose by a bishop. When duly certified they may be exposed for veneration on an appropriate date (for example, fragments of the True Cross on Good Friday, the relics of the saints on their liturgical feasts). It is the custom for the faithful to reverence the relic with a kiss or touch, as with the Veneration of the Cross on Good Friday.

The 'Agnus Dei'

The '*Agnus Dei*' is a sacramental with a long history. It is often associated with relics, and so can be included here.

In fact, it is a simple disc of wax, stamped with an image of the Lamb of God (*Agnus Dei*) and the name of the reigning Pope. Popes traditionally blessed them during the first year of their Pontificate, and every seven years thereafter, and they were made partly with wax from the Paschal Candle used in the Papal Easter liturgies. This close connection with the Papacy, and their comparative rarity, made them much sought after in earlier centuries: you will often find them placed in elaborate frames, like reliquaries, and they can be venerated with a kiss, as with a relic. Though perhaps little known today, they were certainly produced during the Pontificate of John Paul II.

Scapulars

In origin, a scapular is part of the religious habit worn by many orders. It is a long, rectangular piece of cloth with a hole for the head, which hangs down front and back, somewhat like an apron. In religious piety it symbolises the yoke of Christ (*Matthew* 11:30).

The scapular we are considering here is derived from this original form, and can be worn by laypeople. The smaller type of scapular consists of two small pieces of cloth, attached by string and worn over the neck, so that one piece of cloth hangs in front of the body and one behind. Wearing the smaller scapular connects the wearer in some way to the religious order from which the scapular derives – it typically imposes certain obligations on them, and obtains for them certain benefits.

There are many variations of scapular, since many different religious orders have encouraged this form of piety over time. Here we will look at some of the principal types.

The Brown Scapular

"The Brown Scapular of Our Lady of Mount Carmel", associated with the Carmelite Order, is the most well-known. The tradition behind it runs as follows: on 16th July 1251, Our Lady appeared to St Simon Stock, an Englishman, and leader of the Carmelite Order which had recently migrated to Western Europe after being forced to leave the Holy Land by the advance of Islam. St Simon prayed for help for his confreres, and placed them under Our Lady's patronage. Mary herself then appeared to him with the scapular and said, "Take, beloved son, this scapular of thy Order as a badge of my confraternity, and for thee and all Carmelites a special sign of grace; whoever dies in this garment, will not suffer everlasting fire."

To this first promise of Our Lady another was added, known as the 'Sabbatine privilege'. This derives, probably, from the fourteenth century. It states that Our Lady will personally intervene to release from purgatory, on the first Saturday following their death, anyone who has worn the brown scapular, observed chastity and recited the Little Office of Our Lady (or, if unable to read, fasted on the days appointed by the Church and abstained from meat on Wednesdays and Saturdays).

The Church allows these promises to be preached, without entering into the authenticity of the alleged apparitions. However, we must say very clearly that, as with the use of any sacramental, wearing a scapular will only benefit the one who wears it worthily. This means making a real effort to live in holiness of life. It certainly includes regular attendance at Mass, frequent use of the sacraments (especially Confession) and the practice of Christian virtue.

We can now look briefly at some of the other scapulars.

White Scapular

"The Scapular of the Most Blessed Trinity" depicts a red and blue cross, the badge of the Trinitarian Order, founded at the very end of the twelfth century for the ransom of Christians enslaved by the Moors.

Black Scapular

"The Black Scapular of the Seven Sorrows of Mary" is connected to the Servite Order, founded in Florence in the early part of the thirteenth century. The traditions of the order relate that Our Lady herself gave its members their distinctive black habit, saying: "These garments shall be to you a perpetual memory of the sufferings of my heart." The small scapular is derived from this habit and has on its front a depiction of Our Lady of Sorrows.

Blue Scapular

"The Blue Scapular of the Immaculate Conception" originated with the foundress of the Theatine Order of nuns, Venerable Ursula Benicasa, at the beginning of the seventeenth century. The Blue Scapular is worn for the conversion of sinners. In a vision, Christ promised the Venerable Ursula that he would shower blessings on her order, and she asked him to extend these blessings to those who wore the blue scapular.

Red Scapular

"The Red Scapular of the Passion" also has its origin in a vision. Sister Appoline Andriveau, a Daughter of Charity of St Vincent de Paul had a vision of Christ in 1846 in which He promised an increase in the theological virtues (Faith, Hope, and Charity) of those who wore this scapular faithfully and contemplated His Passion. One side of the scapular shows Christ on the Cross, with the words, "Holy Passion of Our Lord Jesus Christ Save us"; the other side shows the Sacred Heart of Jesus and the Immaculate Heart of Mary with the words, "Sacred Hearts of Jesus and Mary, protect us."

Scapular medal

Finally we may note that St Pius X, in 1910, introduced the so-called 'scapular medal', which may be substituted for any cloth scapular approved by the Church. Valid enrollment in the scapulars must, however, be made before the substitution.

Cords

Like scapulars, cords, or cinctures, are worn on the body – in this case passing round the waist. Symbolically they represent chastity – they can also represent attachment to a particular saint, or to a cause.

St Joseph

The cord of St Joseph is a simple cord with seven knots in it – one for each of the seven joys of St Joseph. These are:

1. The Message of the Angel (*Matthew* 1:20)
2. The Birth of Christ (*Luke* 2:7)
3. The Circumcision and giving of the Holy Name of Jesus (*Luke* 2:21)
4. The prophecy of Simeon (*Luke* 2:34)
5. The flight into Egypt and preservation of the Christ Child (*Matthew* 2:14)
6. The hidden life with Mary and Jesus in Nazareth (*Luke* 2:39)
7. The finding of Jesus in the Temple (*Luke* 2:46).

One wears this cord to ask four special graces through the prayers of St Joseph. These are:

1. St Joseph's special protection
2. The grace of chastity
3. Final perseverance
4. St Joseph's particular assistance at the hour of death

St Philomena

Another cord is the cord of St Philomena. It is red and white, in honour of the virginity and martyrdom of the titular saint, and its use was recognised by Pope Leo XIII in 1884. It is worn to implore the grace of chastity.

Medals

Medals are not a form of clothing but are also worn on the person – most usually around the neck. A medal is simply a disc of metal, bearing the image of a saint, or occasionally of Our Lord (for example, the Sacred Heart). Wearing a medal is a reminder, at every moment, of the person depicted – one wears a medal rather as some people like to carry pictures of loved ones in their wallet. It is a sign of an intimate friendship – particularly since the medal is worn around the neck.

One can obtain countless different types of medal, depicting almost every saint in the calendar. Here we will just note two which are particularly popular.

The 'Miraculous Medal'

This medal originates with Sister Catherine Labouré, a novice of the Daughters of Charity in their convent of the rue du Bac, in Paris. She was granted a vision of Our Lady, who told her: 'God wishes to charge you with a mission. You will be contradicted, but do not fear; you will have the grace ... Times are evil in France and in the world. Come to the foot of the altar. Graces will be shed on all, great and little, especially upon those who seek them … I will always have my eyes upon you.' A little later, Catherine was shown another vision, this time depicting a medal. On the one side it depicted Mary, standing on a globe, with rays of light coming from her hands, and around this were the words: "O Mary, conceived without sin, pray for us who have recourse to thee." The whole vision "turned" showing the back of the medal inscribed with the letter "M" entwined with a Cross, and the hearts of Jesus and Mary, the former surrounded with thorns, the latter pierced with a sword. 12 stars circled this oval frame, calling to mind the vision of Our Lady described in the Book of Revelations (*Revelations* 12:1). Catherine understood from this vision that the medal would be a sign of Our Lady's help and protection for all who wore it.

Shortly afterwards the Archbishop of Paris gave approval for a medal to be made according to the model Catherine had seen. Originally known as 'the medal of the Immaculate Conception', it became known as the 'Miraculous Medal' because of a great number of miracles attributed to it. One of the most famous of these was the conversion of Alphonsus Ratisbonne, a wealthy Jewish banker, in 1842. Although he had no intention of becoming a Christian, Ratisbonne agreed to wear one of the newly made medals. Then, visiting the church of St

Andrea delle Fratte in Rome, he had a vision of Our Lady as she is depicted on the medal, and was converted: he subsequently became a priest.

We may also note that one prominent saint of modern times with a great devotion to the Miraculous Medal was the martyr, St Maximillian Kolbe. He founded the *militia Immaculata* to foster devotion to Our Lady and her Son during the years preceding World War II. He subsequently died in the concentration camp at Auschwitz, sacrificing his life by exchanging places with a condemned man.

Catherine Labouré also became a saint. Her body still rests at her convent in the rue du Bac, which is today a beautiful and prayerful shrine at the heart of Paris.

The Medal of St Benedict

This medal is far older than the Miraculous Medal, and is almost equally popular. It bears a cross (among many other symbols) and is named after the Patriarch of Western monasticism, St Benedict of Nursia (+543), who was well known for his devotion to the Sign of the Cross. St Gregory the Great tells us that St Benedict conquered his own temptations by this sign. Another time, when some wicked monks from the monastery of Vico Varo attempted to poison the saint, he made the Sign of the Cross over the cup they offered him, and it broke, exposing their scheme and saving the saint's life. Lastly, it is also said that St Benedict extinguished a fire raging in one of his monasteries by the same Sign of the Cross.

Exactly when this medal was first produced is unclear. It is sometimes associated with Pope Leo IX (+1054), and it was certainly known by the middle of the seventeenth century, when the Sisters of Charity, founded by St Vincent de Paul, wore it attached to their rosary beads. They always retained this devotion to the medal, and for many years in France it was made for them alone. In 1741 Pope Benedict XIV gave his formal approval to the medal, and recommended it to the faithful. It has been particularly popular since 1880, when a special 'jubilee' version was struck to celebrate the 14th Centenary of St Benedict's birth.

Like the Miraculous Medal, the design of the St Benedict Medal is rich in symbolism. On one side we see St Benedict holding his Rule; next to him, on a pedestal, is the cup that once held poison, shattered after he made the Sign of the Cross over it. In very small print above these pictures are the words: *Crux S. patris Benedicti* (The Cross of our Holy Father Benedict). Surrounding the entire face of the medal are the words: *Eius in obitu nostro praesentia muniamur* (May we at our death be fortified by his presence). The reverse of the medal depicts a large cross, in the arms of which are the initials C S S M L - N D S M D, which stand for the rhyme:

Crux sacra sit mihi lux!
Nunquam draco sit mihi dux!
The Holy Cross be my light;
Let not the dragon be my guide.

In the corners of the Cross are the letters C S P D, which stand for the words *Crux S. patris Benedicti* (The Cross of our Holy Father Benedict). Above the Cross is the word "*Pax*" (Peace), the Benedictine motto. Surrounding the entire back of the medal are the initials: V R S N S M V - S M Q L I V B, which also stand for the first words of a rhyme:

Vade retro Satana!
Nunquam suade mihi vana!
Sunt mala quae libas.
Ipse venena bibas!

Begone, Satan,
Do not suggest to me thy vanities!
Evil are the things thou offerest.
Drink thou thy own poison!

Since the most important element of the Medal of St Benedict is a cross, it is often found attached to a crucifix.

Chaplets

A chaplet is another name for a rosary. In origin it is simply a string of beads used for counting prayers, and as such is found in many religious traditions. Even within the Catholic tradition there are several different types, as we shall see below. The use of the chaplet is both very simple and very profound. It allows us to pray in words learnt by heart, while the movement of the beads through the fingers assists us in meditation – the rhythm of words and gestures frees the mind from distractions, allowing it to focus on a religious subject – the 'mystery' which is the subject of our thoughts. Below are some of the better known chaplets.

The Rosary of the Blessed Virgin Mary

By far the most popular of all the chaplets used by Catholics, it is especially associated with the Dominican Order: tradition says that this rosary was first given to St Dominic (+1221) by Our Lady herself, to assist him in his preaching against the Albigensian heresy in southern France. It consists of a circle of beads divided into sets of ten (known as 'decades'). In praying a decade you would say one Our Father, ten Hail Marys and a 'Glory be', while contemplating a particular mystery from the lives of Jesus or Mary. Traditionally, there are fifteen mysteries connected to the Rosary of the Blessed Virgin Mary. These are divided into sets of five:

The Five Joyful Mysteries.

1. The Annunciation
2. The Visitation
3. The Nativity of Christ
4. The Presentation
5. The Finding of the Christ Child in the temple

The Five Sorrowful Mysteries

1. Christ's agony in the garden
2. His scourging at the pillar
3. His crowning with thorns
4. The carrying of the Cross
5. The Crucifixion

The Five Glorious Mysteries

1. The Resurrection
2. The Ascension
3. Pentecost
4. The Assumption
5. The coronation of Mary as Queen of Heaven

In his Apostolic Letter *Rosarium Virginis Mariae* (2002), Pope John Paul II offered five new mysteries as an addition to those listed above. These are:

The Five Luminous Mysteries

1. The Baptism of Jesus
2. The Wedding at Cana
3. The Proclamation of the Kingdom
4. The Transfiguration
5. The Last Supper

Most people say five decades at any one time. In addition, it is usual to begin by saying the Apostles' Creed together with some prayers for the Pope and to end by saying the 'Hail Holy Queen'.

The Rosary of the Blessed Virgin Mary is one of the best loved and most useful of all Catholic devotions. If you would like to explore it further there are many books available, from the CTS and elsewhere, which will help you.

The Rosary of the Seven Sorrows

This chaplet is associated with the Servite Order (see the notes on the black scapular above). It consists of a circle of beads divided into seven sets of seven. In using this chaplet one prays an Our Father and Seven Hail

Marys while meditating on one of the seven sorrows of Our Lady:

1. The Prophecy of Simeon
2. The Flight into Egypt
3. The loss of the Christ Child for three days
4. The Way of the Cross
5. The Crucifixion
6. Christ laid in the arms of Mary
7. Christ buried in the Sepulchre

At the end, one adds another three Hail Marys, in honour of the tears shed by Our Lady during the Passion.

The Franciscan Rosary

This originates in the Franciscan Order, as its name suggests, and is often worn by them as part of their habit. It is similar in appearance to the Rosary of the Blessed Virgin Mary, but is longer, consisting of seven decades rather than five. In praying this chaplet one meditates on the seven joys of Mary:

1. The Annunciation
2. The Visitation
3. The Nativity of Christ
4. The visit of the Magi

5. The Finding of the Christ Child in the temple

6. The Resurrection and appearance of Christ to Mary[5]

7. Mary's Assumption and Coronation in Heaven

The Bridgittine Rosary

This rosary originated with the Order of our Holy Saviour, founded by St Bridget (and known as Bridgettines). It is also worn by the Discalced Carmelites as part of their habit. This chaplet is similar to the Rosary of the Blessed Virgin Mary, except that it consists of six decades. The Joyful, Sorrowful and Glorious Mysteries are said, but with an addition Mystery in each. Thus we have:

The Six Joyful Mysteries

1. The Immaculate Conception of Mary

2. The Annunciation

3. The Visitation

4. The Nativity of Christ

5. The Presentation

6. The Finding of the Christ Child in the temple

---

[5] There is a very old tradition that Our Lady was in fact the first witness to the Resurrection, but that this meeting of Christ and his Mother was private, and not written down in the Gospels.

The Six Sorrowful Mysteries

1. Christ's agony in the garden
2. His scourging at the pillar
3. His crowning with thorns
4. The carrying of the Cross
5. The Crucifixion
6. Christ laid in the arms of Mary

The Six Glorious Mysteries

1. The Resurrection
2. The Ascension
3. Pentecost
4. The Assumption
5. The coronation of Mary as Queen of Heaven
6. The Patronage of Mary

It is obvious that a rosary is primarily intended as an aid to prayer. Sadly, in recent years rosaries have often been used in the secular world as fashion accessories, and worn like necklaces. This is not something a Catholic should do. We can of course carry our rosaries around with us – but they must always be treated reverently.

Items for Use in Church

Almost everything destined for use in the sacred liturgy can be considered a sacramental, and many of these objects are specially blessed and set aside for the purpose. Thus the Church provides official blessings for vestments, altar linens, sacred vessels and so on. As we have already observed, many of these blessing were at one time reserved to the bishop, but can now be carried out by a priest or a deacon.

Role of Sacristan

Perhaps this is a good place to note the important role of the sacristan – the person who looks after all these objects used for worship. Theirs is a vital but often unsung ministry. If we consider that the Church provides a special blessing for all these objects, and considers them holy, we realise that the sacristan is indeed a valuable unit in any liturgical team.

Habits

The distinctive habits worn by many religious orders are also counted as sacramentals, and are often blessed before the 'clothing' of the one who will wear them. Sometimes there is also a customary prayer which may be said each time the habit is put on. Thus even the simple act of dressing takes on a sacred character.

We may note, in this context, that it is the custom in some countries and cultures to set aside a special set of clothes to be worn in church – and priests are occasionally asked to bless them.

Rings

An item of the religious habit with particular significance is the ring worn by many female religious as a sign of their consecration to Christ, the Bridegroom. Of course, it is also a long tradition that the bride (and nowadays, very often the groom) receives a ring at their marriage service. The ring, being round, is an emblem of eternity, and this a most appropriate symbol both of marriage and of religious profession, both of which are intended to last a lifetime. For slightly different reasons, a bishop is also given a ring as part of his episcopal ordination. Here, the ring symbolises the bishop's union with his diocese – he is spiritually 'wedded' to it, and should be prepared to serve and even sacrifice himself for his flock, as St Paul commands husbands to do in the case of their wives (*Ephesians* 5:25). Similarly, an abbot or abbess wears a ring as a sign of their union with the particular community over which they have been placed in authority.

Missals, breviaries, prayer books

Finally, religious books can also be counted among the sacramentals, not only those used in the official worship of the Church (Missals, Breviaries etc) but also prayer books and others which nourish our spiritual lives and lead us closer to God. A prayer provided in the *Book of Blessings* for occasions when a lectern is to be blessed can also to be applied to all such books:

'May God bless you with every heavenly blessing and keep you holy and pure in is sight. May he shower you with the riches of his glory, instruct you with the word of truth, form your hearts with the Gospel of salvation, and enrich you with love for one another, now and for ever. Amen.'

- Sacramental Actions -

Liturgical Gestures

Under this rather broad heading we can include all the movements of the body which we use in the worship of Almighty God. These include:

Sign of the Cross

One makes the Sign of the Cross by touching the forehead and breast and then left shoulder and right shoulder. While doing so one should say (at least mentally): 'In the Name of the Father and of the Son and of the Holy Spirit. Amen.' The Sign of the Cross thus recalls the two central mysteries of our Christian faith – the Holy Trinity and the Redemption (Christ's saving death on the Cross).

A much smaller cross is made when the Gospel is proclaimed at Mass. This cross is drawn with the right thumb over the forehead, lips and breast, while the priest or deacon says the words: 'A reading from the Holy Gospel according to *N.*' The meaning of this gesture is to pray that God's Word be in our mind, on our lips and in our heart.

Genuflection

A genuflection is made by touching the ground with one's right knee, thus halving one's own height. Originally a sign of submission to a king or dignitary, it was adopted by Catholics as the fitting form of reverence when entering the Presence of the Blessed Sacrament. We should always genuflect when entering a church or chapel where the Blessed Sacrament is reserved (unless, of course, physically unable to do so). A bow, whether of the body or head, is not an adequate greeting for Christ, our Lord and God, who is there really present in sacramental form.

Double genuflection (or 'prostration')

This is made by momentarily kneeling, with both knees, while slightly bowing the head. Formerly, it was the prescribed form of reverence to the Blessed Sacrament exposed – as at Adoration or Benediction. It is now an optional form of devotion which many Catholics prefer to retain.

Obviously, in addition to greeting the Blessed Sacrament with a genuflection, we also kneel, both in private prayer and at certain solemn moments of the Mass – especially during the Eucharistic Prayer.

Bows

A bow is made to the altar of a church or chapel if the Blessed Sacrament is not present – it is also made to the celebrant of Mass at certain points, by those assisting in the sanctuary. The *General Instruction of the Roman Missal* instructs the priest to bow his head whenever the holy name of Jesus is pronounced in the liturgy – also at the names of Mary, and of the saint whose feast is being celebrated. It is a very fitting for the faithful to do the same.

Kisses

The celebrant and other sacred ministers reverence the altar with a kiss at the beginning and end of Mass – it is a simple and profound sign of affection and love. The Gospel book is also kissed after the reading has been proclaimed from it. On Good Friday, the cross exposed for veneration is often reverenced with a kiss, and, similarly, the relics of saints when exposed for veneration on their feast day. It is customary to kiss the ring of the Pope when being introduced to him, and also customary – although no longer compulsory – to kiss the rings of bishops and other prelates as a sign of respect and obedience.

Of course one would not want to isolate all these gestures too much from their proper context within the liturgy, as if they had some arcane meaning of their own. On the other hand, seeing them as 'sacramentals' in the proper sense can help us to remember that they are not just rituals, done without thought, but full of real meaning and significance.

Exorcism

A notable effect of sacramentals is their ability to counteract the attacks of evil spirits, who work for our spiritual harm. This is true even of blessed objects (notably holy water), but is especially true of the sacramental action known as exorcism. However, this is such an important subject that it really deserves to be treated in full, and you can read about it more thoroughly in the CTS booklet entitled *Exorcism: Understanding exorcism in scripture and practice* by Fr Jeremy Davies. Here, suffice it to say that the power of the devil is very real (though as nothing compared with the sovereignty of Christ), that we should always avoid exposing ourselves to his influence and should make use of all possible means to draw ever closer to Christ and avail ourselves of his care and protection. The use of the sacramentals is one valuable way in which we can do this, as we shall see.

Blessings

What is a blessing?

The word as used in the Scriptures, especially in the Old Testament, has many meanings. We find there that the original meaning of 'to bless' was to adore and praise God. A secondary meaning is God bestowing benefits on human beings, and it is this sense of 'blessing' which we shall be referring to below. A classic definition of a blessing of this sort was given by the eminent French scholar Fr Baudot in 1935 – a blessing is:

> 'An action accomplished by a man whom the Church has invested with a divine power with the aim of calling down by prayer, divine favour upon persons or things.'[6]

What can be blessed?

We must remember that as Catholics we believe that God's creation, the material world, is good, and not evil. Therefore not only human beings, but almost anything in

---

[6] *Dictionnaire d'Archéologie Chrétienne et de Liturgie.*

creation is potentially capable of being blessed, and used for the glory of God. As *Sacrosanctum Concilium* puts it:

> 'There is hardly any proper use of material things which cannot…be directed towards the sanctification of men and the praise of God.'[7]

In the second part of this booklet we will look at some of the many objects the Church regularly blesses and sets apart for the glory of God and the benefit of his people.

Who can give a blessing?

The definition of Fr Baudot provides us with an answer. A blessing can be given by any person 'whom the Church has invested' with the power to do so. Normally this would refer to an ordained minister, but not always. In fact, the Church's practice has varied somewhat over the centuries. Following the reforms of the Council of Trent, and up until the Second Vatican Council, blessings were contained in the *Rituale Romanum*. Here, many blessings were reserved to the bishop, especially if they concerned objects connected with the liturgy – thus chalices, vestments and many other things could only be blessed by a bishop. Almost all other blessings were reserved to priests. Moreover, some holy objects could only be blessed by the priestly members of certain religious

---

[7] *Sacrosanctum Concilium*, 61.

orders – the Brown Scapular had to blessed by a Carmelite, and the Stations of the Cross by a Franciscan.

Following Vatican II, a general relaxation of all these rules has taken place, which is reflected in the book *De Benedictionibus* (translated into English as the 'Book of Blessings'). Very few blessings are now reserved to the bishop – for example, a priest may now bless vestments, chalices, patens and so forth. Similarly, the old rules which reserved certain blessings to certain religious orders have almost entirely disappeared. In general, the 'Book of Blessings' supposes that a blessing should be given by the person most appropriate in the liturgical context. Thus, if it is a celebration for the whole Diocese, a bishop should be involved. If it is a parish celebration (for instance, the blessing of a couple on their Golden Wedding Anniversary) the parish priest is the appropriate minister. Many blessings can now be given by a deacon (although this should not normally happen if a priest is present). Importantly, the new rules even allow lay people to give blessings too, though in very limited circumstances – most notably, the head of a family may bless his children.

What form of blessing is to be used?

As noted above, the official blessings of the Church are now contained in *De Benedictionibus*. The texts of this book are intended to be used whenever blessings are given (and it is important to observe the correct form provided by the Church, for a blessing to have genuine 'sacramental' significance). However, in practice the situation is a little more complicated. The 'Book of Blessings' is a weighty volume, which the priest will not always have to hand – certainly not, for instance, when asked to bless a rosary or miraculous medal at the end of Mass. For this reason, nowadays, most priests when they receive faculties at ordination are given the authority to bless anything with a simple Sign of the Cross – and this blessing certainly does have 'sacramental' value and conveys it to the object blessed. Most priests will say a few simple words when giving such a blessing. Some also chose to use the forms found in the old *Rituale Romanum*, either in Latin or in translation. As the reader will probably be aware, Pope Benedict XVI has recently moved to grant much wider access to the older liturgical books in his *Motu Proprio Summorum Pontificium*. The Motu Proprio does not specifically refer to the *Rituale Romanum* in the context of blessings, although its use is certainly alluded to.[8] Remembering that Pope Benedict asked pastors to make access to the older liturgical forms available 'when the good of souls requires it', it would seem prudent and charitable to apply this advice to the giving of blessings also.

---

[8] *Summorum Pontificum*, art. 9.

One final point to note: the various forms of blessing have always varied very much according to local custom. Thus, in German speaking lands, it is traditional to bless houses during the Christmas season; but in Italy, and in various other places, it is during the Easter Octave that the parish priest will try to bless the homes of his flock. As an old saying puts it, *nil consuetudine maius* (nothing is greater than custom).

What are the effects of a blessing?

A blessing imparts God's favour, and carries with it the prayers of the Church. It can do this in two different ways. Firstly, those who take part in the service of blessing itself are taking part in a 'sacramental' action, and so they receive the benefits. They may be directly the objects of the blessing (for example, those who receive the blessing of throats on St Blaise's Day, 3rd February), or they may simply be present when a blessing is given (for instance, at the blessing of a new school or parish hall). In the latter case, as long as they consciously participate in the service taking place, uniting themselves to the sacred action, they too will receive benefits from the blessing given. Another way in which blessings can impart God's favour is by giving sacred significance to material objects. These objects themselves are then considered as sacramentals, and the faithful can derive spiritual benefits every time they use them appropriately – for instance, by praying with a blessed rosary or making the Sign of the Cross with holy water.

Conclusion

We said right at the very beginning that the field covered by 'sacramentals' is almost limitless. Perhaps we have already left the reader feeling a little bewildered by attempting to cover as wide an array as possible! On the other hand, there are inevitably other things which have been left out. But writing this little booklet will have been well worth it, if it encourages more people to make use of at least some of the things we have described, and perhaps to appreciate a little more the treasures we very often take for granted. The sacramentals might be seen in one sense as an 'accessory' to our faith – and yet in another way they reflect one of its central tenets. For what could be more natural, for believers in the Incarnation, than that God should choose to share his blessings with us through the everyday things of life?

Index

100 Books you really should read

At last, an ideal pocket guide to 100 good books you really should know about.

Ever wanted to get hold of some really good fiction, biography, history or general spiritual reading to broaden your mind and support your faith? This listing gives a thematic selection with brief review of 100 good books that you should try out. Title and author details are followed by a resume of the book and recommendation as to why you should read it. You can search by title or author. Ranging from great classics to more modern works, this little guide will get you reading!

ISBN: 978 1 86082 526 2

CTS Code: D791